DISCOVERING CANADA

The Great War

ROBERT LIVESEY & A.G. SMITH

Fitzhenry & Whiteside

Published in Canada by Fitzhenry & Whiteside, 195 Allstate Parkway, Markham, Ontario L3R 4T8

Published in the United States by Fitzhenry & Whiteside, 311 Washington Street, Brighton, Massachusetts 02135

www.fitzhenry.ca   godwit@fitzhenry.ca

10   9   8   7   6   5   4   3   2

Library and Archives Canada Cataloguing in Publication
Livesey, Robert, 1940-
      The Great War / Robert Livesey ; illustrated by A.G. Smith.
(Discovering Canada)
Includes index.
ISBN-13: 978-1-55005-136-0
ISBN-10: 1-55005-136-9.—
      1. World War, 1914-1918—Canada—Juvenile literature.
      I. Smith, A. G. (Albert Gray), 1945- II. Title. III. Series: Livesey,
      Robert, 1940- Discovering Canada.

D547.C2L59 2006   j940.3'71   C2006-903247-5

Fitzhenry & Whiteside acknowledges with thanks the Canada Council for the Arts and the Ontario Arts Council for their support of our publishing program. We acknowledge the financial support of the Government of Canada through the Book Publishing Industry Development Program (BPIDP) for our publishing activities.

Illustrations by A.G. Smith
Cover and interior by Janie Skeete, Skeedoodle Design

Printed in Canada

Dedicated with love to veterans
Great Uncle Allen Harts,
Great Uncle Edward Chope Bate,
and
cousins
Shelvey, Clifton, Quinton, Elizabeth, and Andrea.

A special thanks to Dr. James Pauff; Josie Hazen; Linda Biesenthal;
Ian Unwin; Cynthia Perry; Chad Martin, Curator,
Canadian Warplane Heritage Museum, Hamilton, Ontario;
the librarians at the Mississauga Public Library,
Oakville Public Library, and the University of Windsor Library.

Books in the Discovering Canada series:

The Vikings

The Fur Traders

New France

Native Peoples

The Defenders

The Railways

The Loyal Refugees

The Rebels

Black Heritage

The Great War

Contents

ALLIANCES
Allied Powers
Central Powers

NORWAY

North
Sea

SWEDEN

Baltic
Sea

IRELAND

DENMARK

RUSSIA

BRITAIN

NETH.

GERMANY

BEL.

Atlantic
Ocean

FRANCE

AUSTRIA-
HUNGARY

SWITZ.

ROMANIA

Black Sea

PORTUGAL

SERBIA

BULGARIA

SPAIN

ITALY

MN

OTTOMAN
EMPIRE
(TURKEY)

ALB.

GREECE

Mediterranean
Sea

ALLIES' COLONIES

Introduction

 Some people say that nothing is solved by fighting. Others claim that you should stand up and fight for your rights when you are threatened or intimidated.

Most people agree that fighting should be the last resort, used only when every peaceful effort has been exhausted. Conflicts can end in horrific injuries or tragic death. Only fools choose to fight when it is not necessary.

Before the Great War started in 1914, countries in Europe were like kids in a schoolyard. Some were like schoolyard bullies, anxious to fight in order to seize property or to dominate others. But there were no teachers or principals in charge. Larger and stronger nations could defend themselves, but many were too small or weak.

Bullies are not likely to attack someone of their own size or strength. They tend to pick on lone individuals, rather than a group. Sometimes friendships, rather than authority figures, are a better protection from aggressors. Groups of friends can ensure safety.

By 1914, countries in Europe had established agreements, treaties, and alliances for mutual defence. Help from friends was guaranteed if anyone was attacked. Smaller countries depended on protection from larger ones, and most larger ones felt more secure belonging to an alliance. In 1914, the world was filled with rival countries anticipating a fight.

Canada was committed to supporting Britain. During the Great War, more than 600,000 Canadians fought. Almost half were killed or wounded.

1 *Assassination*

Archduke Franz Ferdinand and the Black Hand

The Great War began in 1914 with the assassination of Archduke Franz Ferdinand. The archduke was heir to the throne of Austria-Hungary, a huge empire that included the small province of Bosnia. The archduke was killed in Sarajevo, the capital of Bosnia, where he had travelled with his wife, Sophie, to inspect the Austrian troops stationed in the province.

Just before the assassination, tensions were running high between Austria and its neighbour, the country of Serbia. Serbia wanted to expand its territories, and Austria feared that it might try to take over Bosnia because many Serbs were living there. Between January 1913 and June 1914, the Austrian army had urged an attack on Serbia 25 times. To demonstrate its strength, Austria sent 70,000 soldiers on manoeuvres to Bosnia.

The Black Hand

A terrorist organization, the Black Hand, was created in 1911 with the objective of uniting all Serbs. On June 28, 1914, a motorcade drove down the main street of Sarajevo. The archduke and Sophie were travelling in an open car.

Because they had been warned of an assassination plot, 120 armed policemen were guarding the streets. Six Black Hand terrorists, armed with guns and bombs, were waiting along the route to murder the royal couple.

Terrorist Attack

As the motorcade proceeded to the town hall, a terrorist named Cabrinovic tossed a bomb that bounced off the archduke's automobile and blew up the car behind it. The driver of the royal couple's vehicle quickly sped away.

The archduke ordered the driver to abandon the planned route. The nervous chauffeur turned down a narrow street. General Potiorek, the governor of Bosnia, was in the archduke's car. He screamed at the driver to back up. As the car reversed, another terrorist, Gavrilo Princip, who was by pure chance on the street, ran forward, stepped onto the running board, and fired his pistol point blank. The first bullet hit Franz Ferdinand's neck. The next, aimed at the general, struck Sophie's stomach. Ferdinand and his wife died within seconds.

The Alliances

The deaths of the Austrian royal couple sparked war activity. Because the assassins were Serbian terrorists, Austria declared war on Serbia on July 28, 1914. Serbia was a friend of Russia, which mobilized its army to aid Serbia. France was a friend of Russia, so it also prepared for war. France and Germany had been enemies since the 1870s, when Germany seized the French provinces of Alsace and Lorraine. Germany came to the aid of its friend Austria-Hungary by declaring war against Russia on August 1 and against France on August 3.

Germany invaded the small, neutral country of Belgium because it was the best route to launch an attack on France. Britain had a treaty with Belgium and declared war against Germany on August 4, 1914. Canada and other Commonwealth countries, such as Australia, India, and South Africa, were part of the British Empire. They joined the war to aid Britain.

The five large countries that first started the war were all rich and powerful, all were major steel producers, and all had developed vast railroad transportation systems.

Germany and Austria-Hungary were called the Central Powers. France, Russia, and Britain were the Allied Powers. France, Germany, and Britain had world-wide empires that supplied raw materials and military support. The powerful United States was neutral in the beginning, but it supplied weapons, food, and other materials to the Allied Powers.

Britain's navy was the most powerful. Germany had a strong army and navy, including submarines. Russia had a huge but outdated army.

Great War Alliances

Allied Powers	Central Powers
Russian Empire (until 1917)	German Empire
France	Austria-Hungary
British Empire*	Ottoman Empire
Italy (from 1915)	Bulgaria (from 1915)
Romania (from 1916)	
U.S. (from 1917)	
Serbia	
Portugal (from 1916)	
China (from 1917)	
Japan	
Belgium	
Montenegro (until 1916)	
Greece (from 1917)	

*British Empire included
Canada
Newfoundland (not part of Canada in 1914)
Australia
New Zealand
South Africa
India

2 *Western Front*

Raymond Brutinel, Andrew McNaughton, and Others

The Great War was expected to be over in six weeks, but it got stuck in the muddy trenches of the Western Front and continued for four long, devastating years. It was the first world conflict in which modern weapons, such as tanks, airplanes, submarines, and machine guns, were used along with war tactics and equipment from the past, including swords and cavalry charges.

Germany Invades

The German plan was to capture Paris and force the French to surrender. The fastest route was through the neutral country of Belgium. The king of Belgium, with a small army, slowed down the mighty German forces for 10 days at the city of Liège, which controlled a narrow 20-km pass.

First Battle of Mons and Le Cateau (August 1914)

The invasion of Belgium brought the British into the war. The British army* of 100,000 soldiers, led by Field Marshal Sir John French, reached France by mid-August. The 1st Corps was commanded by General Douglas Haig and the 2nd Corps by General Horace Smith-Dorrien, who faced the German army at the first battle of Mons on August 23, 1914. The Germans forced the British and French armies to retreat. On August 26, the larger German army caught up to Smith-Dorrien's 2nd Corps at Le Cateau. After a six-hour battle, 9000 German and 8000 British were dead or wounded.

* The British later created the First and Second Armies to replace their two corps and, as the conflict continued, expanded to six armies.

Vickers Machine Gun, 1914

Battle of the Marne (September 1914)

After Le Cateau, the French and British continued to retreat. In September, the Germans were advancing close to Paris, but the Allied Powers stopped them at the battle of the Marne. Then it was the Germans who retreated.

First Battle of Ypres (October 1914)

In October, the British pushed the Germans north into Flanders. During the fighting at Ypres, neither side could uproot the other. The European battle line grew until it stretched 765 km, from the Swiss border to the North Sea.

Trench Warfare

Stuck in a stalemate, soldiers on both sides dug, like moles, into the earth to hide from bombardments. Trenches became the battle line for four years.

Opponents faced each other across barren fields, known as "no man's land." If a new recruit peeked over the top of the trench, he could be killed by

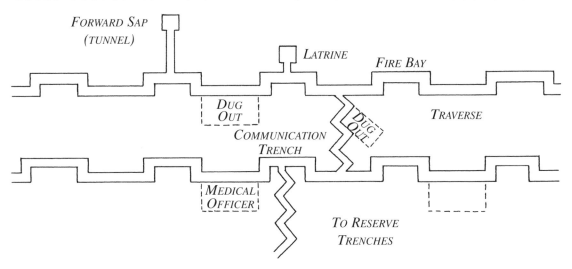

Front Line Trench

FORWARD SAP
(TUNNEL)

LATRINE

FIRE BAY

DUG
OUT

DUG
OUT

TRAVERSE

COMMUNICATION
TRENCH

MEDICAL
OFFICER

TO RESERVE
TRENCHES

enemy snipers, machine guns, or artillery shells. Soldiers piled sand bags at the top of trenches for protection. An average trench would be a metre wide and two metres deep.

Sometimes one side would charge out of its trench, going "over the top" to cross no man's land and capture an enemy trench. Many infantrymen were mowed down by gun fire. If they reached the trenches of their opponents, they fought hand-to-hand, using knives, bayonets, or bare fists. Both sides laid endless coils of barbed wire to prevent assaults.

Trench construction improved, strengthened by wood and iron. Rear trenches housed supplies and communications. Zig-zag patterns were devised. If one trench was captured, the others would not be affected. Cold rains flooded the trenches of Flanders. Troops waded through water and mud up to their knees. Their uniforms, socks, and boots were first soaked by torrents of rain and later frozen in winter snowstorms.

9

Slimy mud, hand-dug toilets, and bodies torn apart by artillery shells attracted flies, fleas, lice, and rats. Disease was rampant. Soldiers spent 10 dangerous days on the front line, then were rotated back to support trenches. Finally, they marched to a rest area, had a shower, and received fresh clothing before returning to the front.

The Princess Pats

On August 4, 1914, when Britain declared war, Canada was instantly involved. Canadians filled the streets, singing and waving flags to celebrate the war. Canada had only 3000 soldiers, but 75,000 militia men.

Prime Minister Robert Borden and his minister of militia and defence, Sam Hughes, went into action. Sam, a soldier-turned-politician, was born in Darlington, Ontario, in 1853. At 13, he joined the militia. At 18, he fought Fenian raiders from the U.S. Colonel Sam, who served in the South African War, was a patriotic, strong-willed man.

A new militia unit, the Princess Patricia's Canadian Light Infantry,* or the Princess Pats, was formed. The 32,000 volunteers sailed to England, eager to see action. Most were British army veterans. They left in October, trained in England, and in six months were on the battlefields.

The newly created force included the Motor Machine Gun Brigade, the Royal Canadian Horse Artillery, and two cavalry regiments.

Canadian Army Corps

The Canadian Army Corps expanded to four divisions, the 1st, 2nd, 3rd, and 4th. The 5th Division, stationed in Britain, mainly replaced the dead. The commanding officer was a British soldier, General Edwin Alderson.

Following the Princess Pats came volunteers from all walks of life: doctors,

* The infantry unit was named after the daughter of the governor general of Canada. She was Queen Victoria's granddaughter.

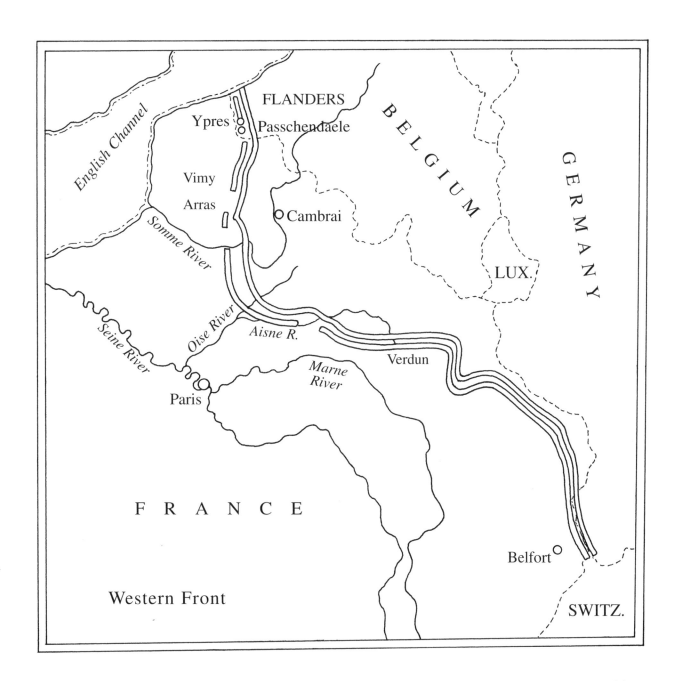

English Channel

FLANDERS

Ypres Passchendaele

BELGIUM

GERMANY

Vimy

Arras

Cambrai

Somme River

LUX.

Seine River

Oise River

Aisne R.

Verdun

Marne River

Paris

FRANCE

Belfort

Western Front

SWITZ.

11

lawyers, labourers, farmers, fishermen, miners, and thousands of boys eager to trade school books for rifles and bullets. Many lied about their age when they signed up, hoping to become heroes on the battlefield.

The infantrymen were hastily trained and issued equipment that had many problems. Each soldier carried his kit on his back. In addition to a Ross rifle, it included a bayonet, steel helmet, great coat, blanket, knapsack, ammunition pouch, gas mask, and a shovel for digging trenches.

The British army had light, comfortable equipment. The bulky Canadian backpack bruised and cut the arms and backs of the recruits. The thick leather chin strap choked them.

The heavy Ross rifle used ammunition that was not available in Europe. It overheated and seized up during battle. It was replaced by the British Lee-Enfield rifle in 1916. The Colt machine guns issued to the Canadians also were replaced by superior Vickers machine guns in 1916.

Canadian army boots were extremely uncomfortable and fell apart after getting soaked in water or mud. The troops nicknamed them "Sham Shoes," a reference to Sam Hughes who supplied them to the army.

The Motor Machine Gun Brigade

In 1905, at age 23, Raymond Brutinel immigrated to Alberta from France, purchased 40 hectares of land, and worked as a prospector. He became a wealthy businessman and predicted the discovery of oil near Edmonton. In France, he had been a captain in the French Army Reserve.

In 1914, Brutinel convinced businessmen to finance a machine gun brigade. When Sam Hughes approved the unit, Brutinel created the 1st Canadian Machine Gun Brigade, known as the Motors. With Major Brutinel in command, it sailed to England with the Princess Pats.

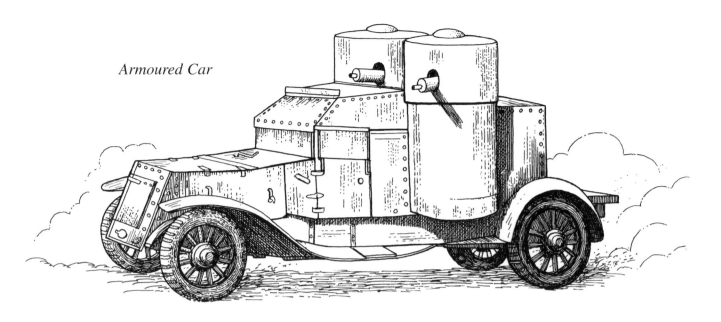
Armoured Car

The Motors consisted of two batteries or units of guns. They had 10 officers, 124 soldiers, 20 machine guns, 8 armoured cars, 8 trucks, and 4 cars. It was the Allies' first motorized armoured fighting unit. Three more Canadian machine gun batteries soon joined them. The Central Powers eagerly employed machine guns. Allied commanders could not see their potential at first. Brutinel invented new tactics and wrote a handbook. In vigorous training, his crews assembled and fired weapons while blindfolded. A machine gun crew of six men discharged 300 bullets a minute. Later, the Motors taught their techniques to Canadian infantry crews. Brutinel convinced the Allied generals to use machine guns as mobile weapons and was promoted to a general by the end of the war.

The Canadian Artillery
Saskatchewan-born Andrew McNaughton was an electrical engineer and an artillery officer in the militia. At 27, he joined the first eager volunteers,

Artillery Gun

distinguished himself in battle, and rose rapidly in rank. He was wounded twice and won a D.S.O.* By 1918, he had become a brigadier general.

The inventive McNaughton developed unique artillery techniques. He deployed "spotters" to report enemy positions to artillery crews. He devised a chain of microphones to detect enemy guns by using sound waves. He created calculation tables to improve the speed and accuracy of gunners. At Ypres in 1915, German artillery devastated the Canadian infantry. By 1917, McNaughton was offering effective protection.

Canadian Cavalry Brigade

In 1915, the Canadian Cavalry Brigade was formed; the commander was General J.E.B. Seely. On February 1, it left for France. Its four regiments were the Royal Canadian Horse Artillery, the Royal Canadian Dragoons, the Lord Strathcona's Horse, and the 2nd King Edward's Horse.**

* Distinguished Service Order
** A British regiment, soon replaced by the Fort Garry Horse from Winnipeg.

14

Christmas Eve (1914)

The Princess Pats arrived in France on Christmas Eve to become part of the British Second Army. The raw recruits learned about war the hard way, in bloody battles where a mistake meant instant death.

Yellow Death: Second Battle of Ypres (April 22, 1915)

The 1st Division of Canadian forces participated in the battle at Neuve Chapelle in March 1915. Later, the troops joined the Princess Pats at Ypres. They were on the left of the British 5th Corps. Left of the Canadians was a French colonial army of African soldiers from Algeria.

On April 22, an ominous, yellow-green fog floated across no man's land. The strange smog slowly enshrouded the trenches. The Africans were the first to be consumed by the eerie mist. They grasped their throats, gasping for air before suffocating. Others floundered as they fled in terror.

The poisonous gas reached the Canadians. Many died a horrible, choking death. Others frantically covered their faces as they met the advancing Germans who followed the deadly haze. In hand-to-hand combat, the Canadians repulsed the attack. On April 24, gas hit them again. Lack of communications created chaos and confusion. The Ross rifles jammed. Surrounded on three sides, the Canucks fought bayonet-to-bayonet. They held their position, but there were 6000 Canadian casualties.

After Ypres, if Allied generals had a difficult assignment, they gave it to Canadians. David Lloyd George* said, "Whenever the Germans found the Canadian Corps coming into the line, they prepared for the worst."

Gas Warfare

Poisonous gas became a new weapon. After the Germans used it at Ypres, the Allies adopted it. The artillery developed gas shells.

* David Lloyd George became the British minister of munitions in 1915.

Soldiers caught in clouds of chlorine gas died slowly of suffocation. Until gas masks were issued, they desperately covered their faces with towels or clothing to keep the chemical out of their lungs. In December 1915, the Germans used a stronger suffocating gas, phosgene.

By July 1917, the Germans had developed mustard gas. It had no odour and caused no damage until 9 to 12 hours after contact. It burned skin off of faces or bodies, created temporary blindness, and destroyed the lungs. Gas masks were also needed for military horses and dogs.

At Passchendaele in 1917, Canadians were subjected to a new horror, sneezing gas. Used in combination with bombs of mustard gas, it seeped through the gas masks, causing sneezing and vomiting. When the victims removed their protection, they exposed themselves to the mustard gas.

Frezenberg Ridge (May 8, 1915)

After the second battle of Ypres, the Princess Pats remained in front line positions for six weeks. Battle fire slaughtered 700 of them.

The commanding officer, Lieutenant-Colonel Francis Farquhar, was killed by a sniper. Major Andrew Gault was wounded. The command fell to Captain H.C. Buller, but a shell sliver hit his eye. Lieutenant Hugh Niven, a young man promoted from a private, became the commanding officer. The Canadians were isolated. Poisonous gas rolled over them, followed by a bayonet charge. They drove the enemy back. Two of their four machine gun crews were destroyed. The battle claimed another 392 casualties. When finally rotated off the front line, only 4 officers and 150 soldiers were alive.

Festubert Disaster (May 15, 1915)

General Haig's First Army attacked Aubers Ridge on May 9. In 12 hours, he lost 11,000 British troops. On May 15, he attacked at Festubert Ridge.

The 1st Division of Canadians joined Haig's army. They were ordered to secure an orchard.* They trudged across open fields of mud, faced deadly fire, suffered terrible losses, but reached their objective.

General Arthur Currie, the commanding officer of the 2nd Brigade, was directed to take a position called K5. The situation was impossible! He begged to delay the attack. General Haig refused. The troops were subjected to merciless machine gun fire. The slaughter continued for five days. Reinforcements were needed to replace the dead. General Seely's cavalry left their horses to fight in the trenches. One-third of the 1st Division died.

Failure at Givenchy (June 15, 1915)

The 1st Canadian Division relieved British troops at Givenchy.

Mines were secretly placed on the front line and detonated as the assault began. The explosions killed some Canadians by mistake. Three 18-pound guns were hauled to the front at night and camouflaged. When they were fired, the guns were spotted and destroyed by enemy artillery. Canadian artillery blasted a path for the infantry through the barbed wire, but enemy machine guns targeted the openings, waiting for them.

Givenchy was a failure. Frontal attacks in daylight meant certain death without machine gun support. When Brutinel's Motor Machine Gun Brigade arrived, it was welcomed by General Alderson, who recognized its value. The Motors trained new infantry machine gun crews.

Massacre at Loos (September 1915)

In September, the British attempted a massive daylight assault at Loos. Thousands of British troops were caught in barbed wire and slaughtered. Canadians had no direct combat role. In the winter of 1915-1916, they formed raiding parties but were not in any major battles.

* Later renamed Canadian Orchard

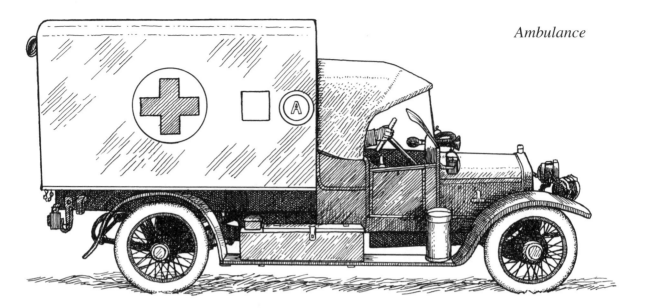

St. Eloi Craters (April 1916)

New Canadian volunteers arrived to form a 3rd Division with what was left of the battle-ravaged Princess Pats. A 4th Division was being planned. In February, the 1st and 2nd Divisions joined British forces in the Ypres area.

The British prepared for six months to attack St. Eloi. Sappers (combat engineers) tunnelled below enemy trenches in order to pack explosives under them. On March 27, the spectacular detonation erupted, producing a barren wasteland of craters that were 10 m deep, 50 m wide, and filled with water. British troops were to capture St. Eloi, and the inexperienced Canadian 2nd Division were to replace them later.

The British got bogged down in the water-filled craters. After a week, the German stronghold was still uncaptured. Plans were changed. The 2nd Division was ordered to complete the job. The Germans counter-attacked. For two weeks, the 2nd Division was riddled by gun fire. The new recruits fought bravely but couldn't take the strong enemy defences.

St. Eloi was blamed on General Alderson, the Canadian commander who took over in a hopeless situation. He was relieved of his command. General Julian Byng, another British officer, took charge of the Canadians.

Guarding Sanctuary Wood and Mount Sorrel (June 1916)

The Canadian Corps, led by General Byng, were on Ypres Ridge protecting Mount Sorrel. The Princess Pats were in Sanctuary Wood. Artillery hit the new 3rd Division, killing the commander, General M.S. Mercer. His assistant, General Victor Williams, was taken prisoner.

The enemy, brandishing bayonets and flame throwers, devastated the Canadians. Others would have surrendered; the stubborn Canadians fought to the death. The Princess Pats lost over 400 men, including their commander, Colonel H.C. Buller. Most of the original volunteers were dead. Replacements, enthusiastic Canadian university students, continued their proud tradition. General L.J. Lipsett of the 2nd Brigade reported that many top officers were dead, the trenches were captured, and entire units were eliminated. The 4th Canadian Mounted Rifles alone had lost 600 men, and there was a 550-m opening inviting the enemy to advance. Brutinel volunteered his mobile 1st Motors to defend the gap. General Currie ordered an artillery barrage that allowed the Canadians to retake their positions.

Bloodshed at the Somme (July 1-November 28, 1916)

The French were fighting at Verdun. On July 1, General Haig began an offensive at the Somme that lasted five months. The first day, there were 57,470 British casualties. The Newfoundland Regiment at Beaumont-Hamel became tangled in barbed wire, like flies in a spider's web. Machine guns ripped their bodies to shreds; 715 soldiers were slaughtered. In July and August, there were over 200,000 British casualties.

Tank

Capture of Flers-Courcelette (September 15, 1916)

The Canadian army added a 4th Division. The 1st Division protected the front line, while the 2nd and 3rd prepared to attack Flers-Courcelette. Bombardments claimed 1000 Canadian casualties before the battle began.

General Byng informed Brutinel of a new, secret weapon called a "landship." Its code name was "water tank"* to confuse enemy spies. In September 1916, 48 tanks were used at Flers-Courcelette.

Brutinel's machine guns and six of the new tanks supported the Canadians. During dozens of attacks and counter-attacks, in ferocious hand-to-hand struggles, the French-Canadian 22nd Battalion established a legacy as unbeatable opponents. An elated General Haig declared that the Canadian gains were the greatest since the start of the Somme.

Wicked weather arrived. On September 26, the 1st Division was ordered to

* "Water tank" was shortened to "tank," a new use for the word in the English language.

take two trenches, named Kenora and Regina. Troops grappled in mud for three days, pulverized by enemy fire. Kenora was captured many times, only to be lost. The 4th and 5th Canadian Mounted Rifles were almost eradicated. Eventually, Kenora was secured.

Despite dozens of attacks, Regina remained impregnable. On October 8, 100 Highlanders tried again. James Richardson, an 18-year-old piper, calmly serenaded the Canadians as they attacked. He died, and was awarded a Victoria Cross. Regina was taken, then lost in a counter-attack.

On October 10, the new 4th Division took over. Pelted by cold rain, the men waded in water up to their knees to occupy part of Regina, but the defenders held them off. Freezing temperatures and snowstorms hampered the inexperienced troops. They finally captured Regina on November 11.

The exhausted Canadians were told to take Desire Trench. Their drenched clothing froze to their numb bodies and cut into their chilled flesh. On November 18, they attacked in snow, sleet, and freezing rain, capturing 600 prisoners. On November 28, the raw recruits of the 4th Division were finally relieved.

Canadian casualties surpassed 24,000. Somme was a bloodbath. On the entire Western Front, 1.25 million soldiers were killed.

Tank Warfare
The tank was produced by the British navy. The British Mark I tank was first used at the Somme. These heavy armoured vehicles moved slower than the troops, at 7 km per hour. They got stuck in the mud and destroyed by artillery, but they terrorized the enemy as they ran over barbed wire and machine gun fire bounced off them. They cleared a path for the infantry. There were "male" and "female" tanks. The larger males carried bundles of logs that they dropped into trenches to create a bridge for them to cross.

Tanks were equipped with machine guns. Later, male tanks had two six-pound guns. At the battle of Amiens in 1918, the Allies had 342 tanks on the first day; 145 were left by the second day; 85 on the third day; 38 on the fourth; and merely 6 by the last day. The Germans captured British tanks and built 20 of their own A7V tanks, with crews of 18 men. France developed and produced 4800 Schneider and Renault tanks.

Ribbon of Cowardice

In the Great War, Norman Bethune left university to enlist. He was wounded, returned to Canada, and completed his medical degree. A woman on a Toronto street approached him and pinned a ribbon of cowardice on his lapel, because he appeared to be a healthy young man who was not fighting in the war. Bethune re-enlisted and served until the war ended.

Dr. Norman Bethune became a hero to millions of Chinese as the Medical Chief of the Red Army during the Chinese rebellion of 1939.

Victim of War

Canada's champion athlete, Tom Longboat, from the Six Nations Reserve in Ontario, became the world's top distance runner in 1909. In "the race of the century" at Madison Square Garden, he beat Alfie Shrubb of England. Tom was escorted by Native chiefs and a red-coated R.C.M.P. officer at the event.

Patriotically, Tom joined the army to fight in the war. He was incorrectly reported as having died in battle. When he returned after the war, he discovered his wife had remarried because of the misinformation.

Christmas Truce

The soldiers on both sides of the war declared a spontaneous cease-fire on December 25, 1914. They emerged from trenches to embrace and celebrate together in no man's land, then returned to fighting the next day.

Poetic Doctor

John McCrae, born in Guelph, Ontario, became a field doctor in the war. At Ypres, his first aid station was engulfed in gas fumes and exploding bombs. Dr. McCrae scribbled his thoughts on a piece of paper.

Later, he visited his friend General Morrison of the Canadian Field Artillery and read the poem he had written. Then he threw it in the garbage. Morrison recovered it, added his own illustrations, and mailed it to *Punch* magazine. In December 1915, the magazine published "In Flanders Fields," the famous poem that is a tribute to soldiers who died in the Great War.

In January 1918, McCrae became ill with pneumonia and died.

Senior Soldier

Sam Steele, born in Orillia, Upper Canada, in 1849, was a soldier all his life. During the fearful Fenian raids, he joined the militia at age 16. In 1870, he marched with the Red River Expedition to end the Riel Rebellion. He joined the North-West Mounted Police and enforced order in the Yukon gold rush. In 1900, he was in South Africa commanding the Lord Strathcona's Horse. By 1915, Sam Steele was a 66-year-old general. He raised, trained, and escorted the Canadian 2nd Division to England.

The Canadian Motors saved thousands of infantry soldiers' lives when they supplied protective and aggressive fire power. But the death toll among the machine gunners was high. One of their nicknames was the Canadian "Emma Gees," another was the "Suicide Club."

Canadian Recipients of the Victoria Cross*
(1914-1918)

Wallace Lloyd Algie, "Billy" Barker, Colin Fraser Barron, Edward Bellew, Philip Eric Bent, Billy Bishop, Rowland Bourke, Alexander Picton Brereton, Jean Brillant, Harry Brown, Hugh Cairns, Frederick Campbell, Lionel "Leo" Clarke, William Clark-Kennedy, Robert Combe, Frederick George Coppins, John Croak, Robert Edward Cruickshank, Edmund De Wind, Thomas Dinesen, Frederick Fisher, Gordon Flowerdew, Herman Good, Milton Fowler Gregg, Frederick Hall, Robert Hanna, Frederick Harvey, Frederick Hobson, Thomas Holmes, Samuel Lewis Honey, Bellenden Hutcheson, Joseph Kaeble, George Fraser "Bobbie" Kerr, John "Chip" Kerr, Cecil "Hoodoo" Kinross, Arthur Knight, Filip Konowal, Okill Learmonth, Graham Thomas Lyall, Thain MacDowell, John MacGregor, Alan McLeod, George McKean, Hugh McKenzie, William Merrifield, William Metcalf, William Milne, Harry Miner, Coulson Norman Mitchell, George Mullin, Claude Nunney, Christopher O'Kelly, Michael O'Leary, Mickey O'Rourke, John Pattison, George Pearkes, Cyrus Peck, Walter Rayfield, James Richardson, Thomas Ricketts, James Peter Robertson, Charles Rutherford, Francis Alexander Scrimger, Robert Shankland, Ellis Sifton, Robert Spall, Harcus Strachan, James Tait, Thomas Wilkinson, Francis Young, Ralph Louis Zengel.

---

* These include men born in Canada or its territories, those who were serving in Canadian forces at the time of their bravery, those living in Canada at the start of the war, and those who came to live permanently in Canada after the war.

Honour a Victoria Cross Recipient

Queen Victoria created the Victoria Cross in 1856 to recognize daring feats of courage performed by British and Commonwealth soldiers or sailors in battle. Since 1856, only 1355 people have received one. During the Great War, 71 Canadians earned a Victoria Cross, many after they had died in battle. Discover more about one of the heroes and honour his bravery in an oral report.

What you need:
- a book about Canadians who have won the Victoria Cross, for example, *Our Bravest and Our Best: The Stories of Canada's Victoria Cross Winners* by William Arthur Bishop (Toronto: McGraw-Hill Ryerson, 1995).
- access to the Internet to research Canadian Victoria Cross recipients

What to do:
1. Choose one of the Canadians awarded a Victoria Cross (see page 24).
2. Research the bravery that he showed to deserve the award. List the 10 most important or most interesting facts in point form on a card that you can refer to as you speak.
3. Present a short oral report to your friends or classmates explaining what the hero did to deserve the award. Tell the story in an enthusiastic, interesting style that will honour the bravery of the individual and capture the imagination of your audience. If you have access to props or photos from the Great War, display them as you talk.

3 *Eastern Front*

Joe Boyle, Lawrence of Arabia, and Others

What started as a European war expanded to battlefields around the world and armies from five continents. The war on the Eastern Front was different from the war on the Western Front.

Russia was an ally of Britain and France. It had a huge army, but its infantry and cavalry were no match for the new machine guns and air power of Germany and Austria.

Battle of Gumbinnen (August 20, 1914)

German generals miscalculated the time that it would take Russia to prepare for war. They estimated 10 weeks. The Russian First Army, led by General Paul von Rennenkampf, was ready in 10 days. It attacked eastern Germany and won a clear victory at the battle of Gumbinnen, causing the Germans to retreat. Russia created a second war on the Eastern Front.

Battle of Tannenburg (August 1914)

A second Russian army, commanded by General Alexander Samsonov, also moved into action. The Central Powers had to pull three army corps from the West and redeploy them in the East. This contributed to the Allied victory on the Western Front at the battle of the Marne River in 1914. Without the Russian offensive, France might have fallen early in the war.

A message from General von Rennenkampf to General Samsonov was intercepted. The Germans discovered the positions of the Russian armies.

They moved their powerful army south by railroad and crushed the Russians, commanded by Samsonov, at Tannenburg.

Forced into a swamp, the Russian army was destroyed. One Cossack cavalry brigade of 500 dashing riders on magnificent white horses were pressed together so tightly that, after being slaughtered by machine guns, the corpses of both men and animals were left in a standing position. The Germans lost 13,000 men, compared to 125,000 Russians. General Samsonov, dismayed by the horrific disaster, committed suicide.

Within weeks, the Germans confronted General von Rennenkampf, killing another 100,000 Russian soldiers.

The Russians recovered. In September, they delivered a deadly blow against the Austrian army in East Prussia, killing more than 300,000. In October, they forced the Germans to withdraw from Poland.

The Pacific

The Great War expanded into the Pacific. The Allied goal was to control the ocean trade by capturing the colonies and ports of the Central Powers. From the beginning, Japan had been a member of the Allied Powers. On August 23, 1914, it conquered the German colonies of Caroline and Marshall islands in the Pacific Ocean. Joined by British and Indian troops, the Japanese invaded the Chinese port city of Qingdao, which was occupied by German forces. On August 30, New Zealand captured the German island of Samoa. Within a month, Australia occupied German New Guinea.

Africa

In August 1914, the French and British captured Togoland. In September, South Africa attacked German South West Africa. The Germans repulsed an attack from Indian and British forces in East Africa.

Middle East

In November 1914, Turkey joined Germany. The Dardanelles, the entrance to the Mediterranean, was blockaded. German cruisers raided Russian ports on the Black Sea. Turkey tried to invade Russia, but 30,000 soldiers froze to death in the Caucasus Mountains. The Turks attacked the Suez Canal and attempted to invade India via Afghanistan. Britain defended the canal and colonies. Turks killed 500,000 Armenians thought to be Russian supporters.

Gallipoli

In April 1915, British, Australian, and New Zealand troops tried to break the blockade of the Dardanelles by assaulting the Gallipoli Peninsula. The Turks controlled the hills and stopped them on the beaches. A second attack was also squashed. Cholera and malaria plagued Allied forces in the hot summer. A bitter, cold winter forced them to retreat after nine months.

Mountain War

In May 1915, Italy joined the Allies and attacked Austria-Hungary. The struggle was in the majestic, snow-covered Alps. A stalemate developed as 15 Italian divisions made slow progress against 5 Austrian divisions on the heights above. From June to August, there were 11 battles that gained only 11 km at the cost of 250,000 casualties. Alpine troops climbed sheer cliffs and carved caves into the rocky mountain sides 3 km above sea level. Austrians dropped grenades onto Italians who were drilling tunnels to plant explosives. For two years, the front line in the mountains remained unchanged.

Bulgaria joined the Central Powers in October 1915 and then invaded and occupied Serbia in two days. The Serbian army and refugees retreated in a tragic exodus across cold, barren mountains to escape to Albania. Half the army of 200,000 soldiers and a very large number of civilians perished.

Desert War

In 1914, the British developed three desert fronts against the Turks. A large British force advanced from Egypt to Palestine, eventually capturing Jerusalem on December 9, 1917. A second British-Indian army moved from the Persian Gulf and slowly conquered Mesopotamia (present-day Iraq). In November 1915, the Turks counter-attacked. The British retreated to Kut-al-Amara. Hunger and disease killed thousands. A British division of 9000 troops surrendered to the Turks. Baghdad was finally taken in March 1917.

Lawrence of Arabia

The third desert front involved British Colonel T. E. Lawrence, who became famous as Lawrence of Arabia. He spoke Arabic and convinced Emir Faisal and other Arab leaders to revolt against Turkey in June 1916. Leading an Arab army of 10,000 across the desert, Lawrence pushed the Turks out of Hejaz, then helped the British take Jerusalem.

Adversities for the Allies (1915-1916)

The Germans pushed the Russians out of Poland, Estonia, Latvia, and Lithuania. The battles at Verdun and the Somme were great losses. Irish nationalists received weapons from Germany to rebel against the British.

Russia to the Rescue

Russia aided the Allies by invading Turkey. A Russian general, Alexei Brusilav, attacked Austria in June 1916 and, after 20 engagements, was victorious. Unlike troops on the Western Front who huddled in trenches for years, the Russians advanced 160 km in a month and captured 250,000 prisoners. Russia also defeated the Central Powers in the Balkans. Trains filled with German troops roared from the Western Front to confront Brusilav, who

Mediterranean Sea

PALESTINE

Jerusalem

Mosul

MESOPOTAMIA

Tigris R.

Baghdad

PERSIA

Kut

ANAZAH

SHAMMAR

Basra

KU

HEJAZ

EGYPT

Red Sea

NEJD

ARABIA

IDRISI

IMAM

N

AFRICA

HADHRAHAUT

ADEN

Gulf of Aden

retreated. The Russian victories cost 6.7 million casualties. In September 1915, Tsar Nicholas took personal command of Russia's army.

Revolution in Russia

With the tsar on the battlefield, his wife and the "mad monk" Rasputin were in charge of the country. Strikes and demonstrations broke out. Instead of squashing the riots, soldiers deserted. Russia was in chaos. On March 15, 1917, Tsar Nicholas was forced to abdicate. A provisional government was established. The Germans encouraged the domestic unrest and revolution by smuggling the communist leader, Vladimir Lenin, into Russia. The Russian people supported the communist revolt against the royal family. War became impossible because of the change in Russian leadership.

Joe Boyle: Uncrowned King of Romania

Joe Boyle was born in Toronto in 1867 but grew up in Woodstock, Ontario. He preferred to ride horses rather than go to school. At 17, he disappeared, leaving a simple note: "Gone to sea. Don't worry about me. Joe."

Joe returned from sea at age 21. He got married to an American woman, was a successful merchant, owned a home, and had four children.

At age 30, Joe left his wealth and family to travel to the Klondike gold-fields in Yukon territory. Dawson City in 1898 was a wild, wide-open town. Joe arrived with only 50 cents. He earned money as a boxer and bouncer. Klondike sourdoughs panned for gold on small creek-bed claims with frontages of 150 m. Joe convinced the government to grant him a huge frontage 13 km long. It was the greatest mining coup of the day.

When war broke out in 1914, Joe was a millionaire but, at age 47, too old for service. So he financed the Yukon Machine Gun Battery.

Boyle travelled to London where he was named a lieutenant-colonel. The

British found the perfect challenge for his talents. Russia's trains couldn't move. The country was in the midst of both winter and the communist revolution. Supplies and food were needed desperately on the Eastern Front. Colonel Boyle accepted the assignment and mobilized the Russian trains.

Joe Boyle travelled on to Romania, a small, starving country squashed between German and Russian troops. There Joe met English-born Queen Marie, who had persuaded her husband to join the Allies. Joe dedicated the rest of his life to helping Romania and its queen.

In 1917, the communists seized power in Russia, where the Romanian royal treasury was stored for safety. In Moscow, Joe commandeered a train. Attacked by communist rebels, he drove the locomotive himself. The gigantic Canadian, with badges of Klondike gold on his khaki uniform and wearing cavalry boots, returned the royal fortune to Queen Marie.

Joe Boyle issued his own orders. On one adventure, he sailed across the Black Sea to rescue Romanian hostages. On another, he visited the imprisoned Tsar Nicholas II, and offered to help him and his family escape. The tsar refused. Within six months, the entire royal family was executed.

When the war ended, Joe Boyle stayed in Romania as the companion of Queen Marie. The chivalrous Canadian colonel's romantic attachment to her gained him the title of the Uncrowned King of Romania.

In 1918, Joe suffered a stroke that left him paralyzed. He retired to the home of a Yukon friend living in England. During his absence from Canada, his gold business collapsed. He died in 1923, a penniless invalid.

Queen Marie designed the headstone for his grave. On it was her name, Marie, and one of Joe Boyle's favourite lines from Robert Service's poem "The Law of the Yukon":

> A man with the heart of a Viking
> And the simple faith of a child.

Make a Multicultural Force

Troops from many of the countries of Europe and their colonial empires participated in the Great War. Make your own multicultural force.

What you need:
- scissors
- crayons or coloured pencils
- white glue
- bristol board

What to do:
1. Photocopy pages 34 and 35.
2. Colour the soldiers before cutting them out. Use your library and the Internet to research the uniform colours.
3. Cut the bases from bristol board using the oval pattern on page 35.
4. Cut out the soldiers, fold back the tabs, and glue them to the bases.

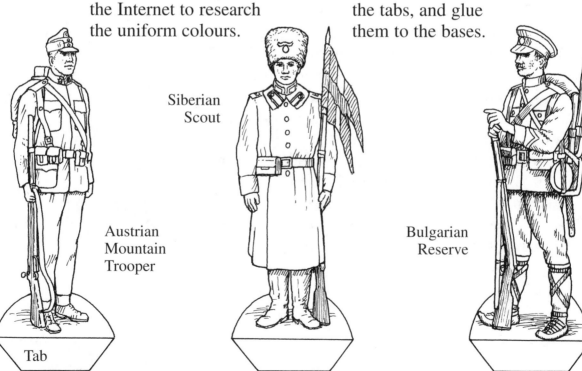

Austrian Mountain Trooper

Siberian Scout

Bulgarian Reserve

Tab

Cameroon
Soldier

Base

Tonkinese
Soldier

French
Infantry

Indian
Cavalry

Highland
Soldier

35

CHAPTER 4 *Home Front*

Beth Smellie, Mabel Adamson, Mata Hari, and Others

A war is like an iceberg. Only 10 percent of an iceberg shows above the surface; the other 90 percent that supports it is hidden below. In the Great War, the Canadian warriors on the front line were supported by millions of women, children, and other civilians who sweated and sacrificed on the home front.

Women at War

The Great War dramatically changed the lives of women in Canada, as it did in all countries on both sides. They substituted for fathers, husbands, and sons on farms, in factories, family businesses, and in communities and homes. They operated all forms of transportation and serviced the roads. Some toiled in coal mines. Their working hours increased as they took over men's work.

Factory work had been mainly a male occupation; when the Great War started, women suddenly became factory labourers. In some countries, it became illegal to employ men if women could do the factory jobs. The pay was low, and the work was often unhealthy. Some women worked in factories that had toxic gas fumes or were contaminated by lead, copper, and nickel. Oil spots, caused by oil dripping from machines, appeared on their skin. Their long hours and strenuous work created accidents. Pregnant women and their babies were endangered.

Covering airplane wings in a factory

Canary Crew

Over 30,000 Canadian women produced shells and weapons in munition factories. Some "Munitionettes" who came into contact with TNT dust developed a sickly, yellow skin condition, which earned them the nickname of the Canary Crew. Others became infected with tuberculosis or similar deadly diseases caused by unhealthy working conditions. General Joffre, the French commander-in-chief, declared: "If all the women factory workers stopped for twenty minutes, the Allies would lose the war."

Women's Auxiliary Army Corps (WAAC)

It was rare for women to fight in battles, but many joined auxiliary armies. Women clad in army khaki worked as cooks, administrative clerks, secretaries, carpenters, mechanics, and truck drivers. A woman in the WAAC was called "the girl behind the man behind the gun."

Legion of Death

In Russia, armed female soldiers fought on the front lines. Russian women formed the first battalion from Petrograd,* called the Legion of Death. Many died during a Russian retreat, but they captured over 100 German soldiers. They were respected and feared by both allies and enemies.

Fund Raising

Women raised money for the Canadian Women's Hospital Ship Fund and the Red Cross. The Canadian Patriotic Fund raised $43 million and the Victory Loan campaigns sold posters and postcards worth $1.7 million.

Children at War

There were no laws to keep children in school. Twelve-year-olds worked in factories for 14 hours, day and night, Sundays and holidays.

Food had to be produced for the army and the nation. Children, the elderly, and other civilians laboured on the farms, planting and harvesting the crops. The Soldiers of the Soil movement encouraged more than 25,000 city school boys to work on farms in the summer. The Ontario Farm Service Corps issued badges to over 7000 boys and 1300 girls who worked in the fields to support Canada's Campaign for Greater Food Production.

Young girls knitted socks for soldiers. Children sold patriotic tags on a total of 64 Tag Days. The Rural Schools Patriotic Fairs sold pins.

* St. Petersburg today

Canadian Bluebirds

Canadian Nursing Sisters, called Bluebirds, served overseas as army officers in perilous places and overcrowded military hospitals. In Europe, private automobiles were turned into ambulances and mansions were converted into hospitals.

More than 2500 Canadian women in the Army Nursing Service travelled to Europe. Over 40 of the Medical Corps nurses died heroically while supplying aid on the front line.

Nurse Helen Fowlds of Hastings, Ontario, enlisted immediately in 1914, and by February 1915, she was part of the Canadian Army Medical Corps. She served in France, Egypt, Malta, and Greece. Helen battled a chronic respiratory infection and bronchitis but recovered and returned home.

Beth Smellie from Port Arthur, Ontario, served in the Great War and later in the Second World War. She became chief superintendent of the Victorian Order of Nurses, matron-in-chief of the Royal Canadian Army, and the first woman colonel in the Canadian Army.

Changing Society

The Great War caused dramatic social changes. Women labourers led strikes, demanding equal pay, better working conditions, and the right to vote. In 1916, women were voting in provincial elections in Alberta, Saskatchewan, and Manitoba, and a year later in British Columbia and Ontario. In Quebec, women couldn't vote until 1948. The Wartime Elections Act of 1917 let only the sisters, wives, and daughters of soldiers vote. In 1918, all women over the age of 21 could vote in federal elections.

Before the war, no Canadian paid income tax. To help finance the war, politicians declared a drastic temporary tax based on everyone's income. It was to exist only while Canada was at war, but the tax on income was never removed. Today, some Canadians pay more than half their salaries as tax to federal, provincial, and city governments.

The concept of Daylight Savings Time began in the Great War. It was designed to maximize the factory production time on the home front.

Before the war, men's hair was worn long. After soldiers in the trenches shaved their heads to avoid lice, short hair became stylish for men. The Beatles re-introduced long hair in the 1960s, but the military cut had become popular again by the 1990s.

Forced to Fight

Prime Minister Robert Borden visited Canadian casualties suffering from missing limbs, horrific burned bodies, and shell shock. He felt it was unfair for other men to refuse to serve their country.

On August 29, 1917, Parliament passed the Military Service Act. It was the beginning of conscription, or compulsory military service. Soon, 46,000 conscripts were forced to fight in the war. The policy divided the country. Most of English Canada supported Britain and the war, but many French-speaking

Canadians felt no loyalty. In March 1918, the arrest of a French-Canadian objector caused rioting in Quebec.

Mabel Adamson

When her husband went off to war with the Princess Pats, Mabel Adamson followed him to England and became active in the Belgium Soldiers Fund. Along with another Canadian, Kathyrn Innis-Taylor, Mabel created the Belgium Canal Boat Fund, which raised money to transport supplies down the canals to 10,000 Belgium families isolated behind enemy lines.

Spies

Spies intercept messages sent by radio and telegraph. In the Great War, both sides protected their communications by using elaborate codes and used code-breaking, or cryptography, to decipher intercepted information. In 1917, British spies deciphered the Zimmermann telegram sent by the Germans to Mexico, which invited Mexico to join the Central Powers and attack the U.S. This encouraged the U.S. to declare war in April 1917.

English-born Edith Cavell was working as a nurse in Belgium when the Germans occupied Brussels in August 1914. She stayed on, offering medical aid to 200 British troops who had been captured. She was accused of helping some to escape. In 1915, she was shot by a firing squad.

Winnie the Pooh

Children's stories about Winnie the Pooh were created after the author visited a black bear named Winnie in the London zoo. The bear cub came from Canada with Captain Harry Colebourn as the mascot of the 2nd Canadian Infantry Brigade. Winnie was named after the captain's home of Winnipeg.

Mata Hari

Mata Hari was the stage name of Margaretha Zelle, a Dutch entertainer. Dressed as a princess from Java, she became famous throughout Europe as a dancer. While performing in Paris in 1914, she was recruited by the French Secret Service and sent to Spain. The beautiful dancer seduced high-ranking German officers in order to obtain military information for the French.

When Mata Hari returned to France, she was arrested. She was accused of being a double agent who deliberately supplied incorrect information to the French. Some people say she was double-crossed by a German officer who gave her the false information. In October 1917, she was executed by a French firing squad.

43

During the Great War, over 500,000 pigeons delivered military messages, which were attached to their legs. Some were parachuted in boxes to drop zones in occupied territories and kept until released by spies. Others were sent by reconnaissance pilots. The Germans used small "Pigeon Post" forms of lightweight paper. Longer messages were photographed and reduced 300 times to microdot size.

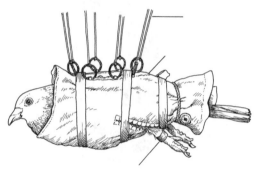

James Bond 007

The fictional James Bond was based on a real British secret service agent from the Second World War. Born William Samuel Clouston Stanger in Winnipeg in 1897, he later became William Stephenson and was known as Intrepid. The spy training camp depicted in the movies existed near Lake Simcoe in Ontario.

During the Great War, William joined the Canadian Army Engineers. He was promoted to sergeant at age 18, and was gassed in 1916. He recovered and joined the Royal Flying Corps. William was shot down and captured by the Germans. He was awarded the Distinguished Flying Cross, the Military Cross, the *Croix de Guerre*, and the *Legion d'Honneur*.

Write a Coded Message

To prevent spies from obtaining vital information, soldiers and civilians wrote coded messages during the Great War.

Imagine you are a politician sending a message to an ally, a general issuing an order, a soldier writing home from the trenches, a woman or child in Canada communicating with a husband or father on the front line in Europe, or a spy reporting to a superior in the secret service.

What you need:
- paper and pen or computer

What to do:

1. With a partner, create a secret vocabulary to substitute for military terms, such as army, battle, enemy, or ship. Use musical terms, names of plants, animals, friends, relatives, automobiles, etc.

2. Devise a hidden code with your partner. For example, every fifth word in your letter could be part of the hidden message. Make your code as difficult or complex as possible.

3. Invent a short, simple secret message. Examples: "Attack from the west," "Our Division moved to the front at Ypres," "Our factory doubled production by creating a night shift."

4. Create a normal letter, disguising the secret message.

5. Have your partner decipher the letter and reply in code.

6. Exchange letters written by other partners. Can you break their code and decipher it?

5 *U-Boats and Battleships*

Admiral Jellicoe, Admiral Scheer, and Others

On August 4, 1914, the dockyard in Montreal was shut down because of the danger of German war ships. The Royal Canadian Navy (RCN), newly created in 1910, had only 350 sailors and two armoured cruisers, HMCS *Niobe* and *Rainbow*. British Columbia purchased two submarines to patrol and protect the Pacific coast. The RCN later purchased them, but they never saw any action.

Britain Ruled the Sea

The British navy, the most powerful in the world, prevented German vessels from leaving their ports. In the first six months of the war, Britain destroyed or captured 383 enemy ships and forced 788 into neutral ports.

German Raiders

One German battle cruiser, *Goeben*, and 14 other light cruisers were at sea before the British blockaded German ports. They became daring, dangerous raiders, attacking Allied ports and ships, and then rapidly disappearing. When Turkey joined the Central Powers in 1914, the *Goeben* and another cruiser made raids on Russian ports in the Black Sea.

In the Far East, a German squadron of raiders survived. The *Emden* ran raids in the Indian Ocean, until the Australian cruiser, *Sydney*, sank it in November 1914.

An accidental explosion destroyed one German cruiser off the coast of

Brazil, but raiders sank four British war ships along the coast of Chile on November 1. On December 8, at the Falkland Islands, the British destroyed all the German raiders in the South Atlantic. By April 1915, all German raiders had been eliminated or forced to take cover in neutral ports, but they had sunk 54 British ships.

U-Boats

At the start of the Great War, boats that could travel underwater were a new invention. The British navy controlled the surface, but the Germans quickly produced a massive new fleet of U-boats. The term comes from the German word *Unterseeboot*, which means "undersea boat." Instead of names, they were given numbers that followed the letter U, as in U-37.

U-boats were uncomfortable, but easy to manoeuvre. The space inside was compact and tight. The heat and fumes from the engines were suffocating. The U-boats terrorized the Allies, as they torpedoed war ships.

U-boats sank 5554 commercial vessels. Many were neutral American merchants delivering supplies to the Allies. Crews of the U-boats were also at risk; 178 German U-boats were bombed, destroyed by minefields, or torpedoed.

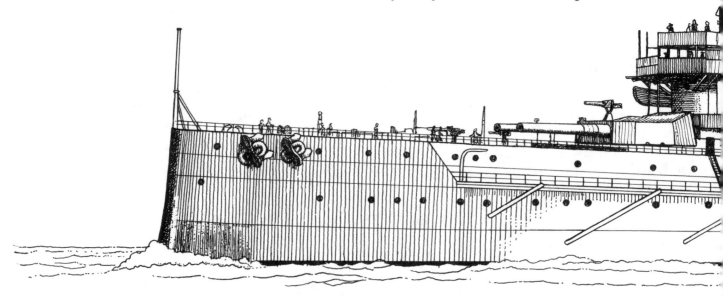

First Aircraft Carrier

The British created the first aircraft carrier in order to attack U-boat and Zeppelin bases. By 1918, seven *Sopwith Camels* were flying from HMS *Furious*. Sea planes also bombed and torpedoed enemy ships.

Convoys

To guard against U-boats, commercial ships began travelling in convoys, protected by war ships such as cruisers. Observation balloons detected the U-boats and smoke screens protected the convoy. If attacked, convoys retaliated with cannons, depth charges, and torpedoes.

Dazzle, Decoys, and Dreadnoughts

Strange patterns and bizarre designs, called dazzle camouflage, disguised 2700 merchant ships and 400 escorts. Other protection included minefields and decoy boats that attracted and trapped the deadly U-boats.

Both Britain and Germany built gigantic, super dreadnoughts, which were protected by armour plates. German ships were equipped with 380-mm guns that could fire one-tonne shells every minute. The German guns could shoot longer distances and were more accurate than the British.

Battle of Jutland

Admiral John Jellicoe commanded Britain's Grand Fleet; Admiral Reinhardt Scheer commanded Germany's High Seas Fleet. Both were wary of having their ships destroyed. There was only one major sea battle.

On the night of May 31, 1916, Admiral Scheer defied the British blockade and moved the entire German High Seas Fleet into the North Sea, at the southern tip of Norway. The British confronted him in what became known as the battle of Jutland, off the coast of Denmark.

The rivals clashed in a mammoth display of fire power. Britain had 28 gigantic dreadnoughts and 9 battle cruisers; German ships were led by 16 dreadnoughts and 5 battle cruisers. Guns flashed and ships exploded. By morning, the battle had ended. The Germans lost a battle cruiser, a dreadnought, four light cruisers, and five destroyers. More British ships were destroyed: three battle cruisers, four armoured cruisers, and eight destroyers. Among the dead were 6094 British sailors and 2551 German sailors.

The British claimed the victory because the German fleet was forced back into its ports. It escaped by creating a smoke screen and covering its retreat with a deadly volley of 28 torpedoes. Britain continued the blockade. Both fleets avoided another major encounter for the rest of the war.

Decorated U-Boat

The Iron Cross was a medal awarded to Germany's military heroes, similar to the French *Croix de Guerre* and the British Victoria Cross.

In 1915, when the German U-9 submarine successfully torpedoed many British war ships, the German captain, Otto Weddigen, was allowed to paint an Iron Cross on his U-boat.

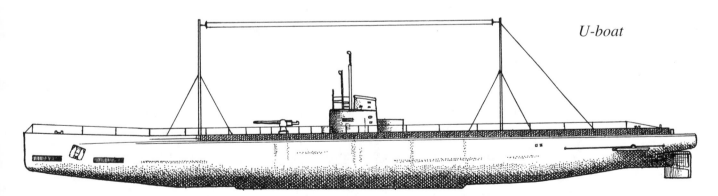

U-boat

Halifax Explosion

Canadian Merchant Marines manned British ships crossing the Atlantic Ocean in large convoys to deliver food and military supplies. In three winter months of 1917, 800 ships were sunk by U-boats and 8000 sailors died.

Thousands of ships moved in and out of the Halifax harbour. On December 6, 1917, the Norwegian ship, SS *Imo* collided with the French vessel SS *Mont Blanc*, which carried 2268 tonnes of explosives. The devastating explosion destroyed not only other ships and crews but a vast area of Halifax and Dartmouth. A total of 1950 men, women, and children lost their lives and 9000 were injured. The explosion flattened homes, factories, and businesses, causing $35 million in damage. It was the greatest human-created catastrophe in world history at that time.

Revenge for the Llandovery Castle

In July 1918, the Canadian hospital ship, *Llandovery Castle*, was sunk, killing all but 24 people. As the Canadian divisions gathered in the first week of August to attack at Amiens, they were anxious to seek revenge. They used the ship's name as code words to report to their headquarters.

Sinking of the Lusitania

In May 1915, a U-boat sank the passenger ship *Lusitania*. The 1198 civilians who drowned included 128 American citizens. Anti-German sentiments erupted throughout the U.S., and the Germans promised to follow "cruiser rules" in the future. That meant that they would warn a ship and allow the passengers to escape in row boats before destroying the vessel. But, by early 1916, the U-boats had stopped warning civilian ships.

Although the neutral American merchant ships were supplying the Allies with food and war materials, the U-boat attacks were a major reason for the U.S. declaring war on Germany on April 6, 1917, and on Austria-Hungary on December 7, 1917. Also, British spies intercepted the telegram from Arthur Zimmermann, the German foreign secretary, inviting Mexico to become a partner with Germany by attacking the U.S. President Wilson claimed that America had to "make the world safe for democracy."

Changing Names

In early June 1915, Field Marshal Lord Kitchener, the British secretary of state for war, sailed on HMS *Hampshire* to consult with the tsar of Russia and his top army officials. He drowned when the ship hit a mine off the Orkney Islands and sank. The town of Kitchener, Ontario, previously called Berlin, changed its German name for an English one, like many other communities in Canada.

When the U.S. declared war on Germany in 1917, American hamburgers, originally named after the German town of Hamburg, were renamed "liberty sandwiches" during the war.

Make a Periscope

Periscopes were used in submarines and also in the trenches to peer over the top without being seen.

What you need:
- glue
- ruler
- 2 mirrors
- black paint
- 2 sheets of white bristol board

What to do:
1. On one sheet of bristol board, draw the outside view. Cut it out and fold the tabs.
2. Turn it over and draw the inside view.
3. Paint the inside black. Do not paint tabs or mirror panels.
4. Using the second sheet of bristol board, draw and cut out the top, bottom, mirror panels, hood, and visor.
5. Glue the two mirrors to the mirror panels.
6. Fold the tube panels around the mirror panels. Glue panel A along the tab on panel D.
7. Glue the top and bottom panels, hood, and visor.

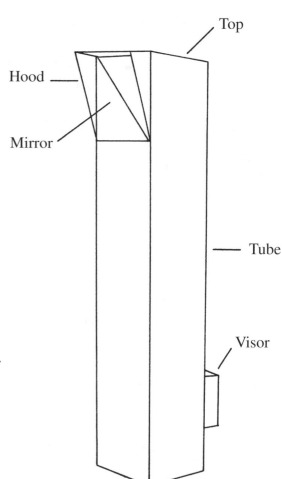

54

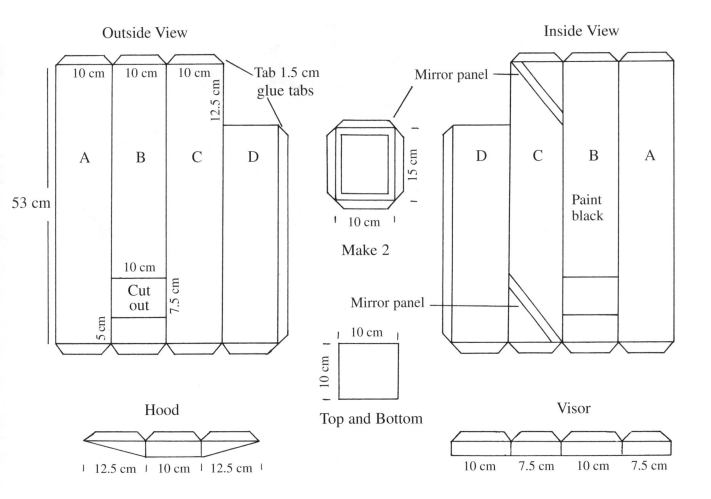

Outside View

| 10 cm | 10 cm | 10 cm | Tab 1.5 cm glue tabs |

A   B   C   D

53 cm

12.5 cm

10 cm
Cut out

7.5 cm

5 cm

Hood

12.5 cm   10 cm   12.5 cm

Inside View

Mirror panel

Make 2

10 cm

15 cm

D   C   B   A

Paint black

Mirror panel

Top and Bottom

10 cm

10 cm

Visor

10 cm   7.5 cm   10 cm   7.5 cm

6 Flying Aces

CHAPTER

Billy Bishop, Billy Barker, and Others

Because Canada had no air force in 1914, the only way a Canadian could become a pilot during the Great War was to join the British Flying Corps. The British Flying Corps became the Royal Air Force, recognized as a third military fighting force, equivalent to the army and navy.

Four of the top 12 Flying Aces in the Great War were Canadian pilots.

Flying Machines

The first flying machines were invented only 11 years before the Great War. In Canada, telephone inventor Alexander Graham Bell designed flying machines with J.A.D. McCurdy, Casey Baldwin, and Thomas Selfridge. Selfridge designed the Red Wing, which flew in 1908. McCurdy and Baldwin tried to convince Canada's minister of militia and defence, Sam Hughes, of the airplane's military value, but he said it "will never play any part in such a serious business as the defence of a nation."

Airplanes were untested in battle, but by the end of the war, more than 20,000 had been built. Early planes were small, constructed of wood and canvas, and had a top speed of only 100 km per hour. They were used at first to photograph enemy positions and to radio news about troop movements. Soon pilots began to drop bombs and grenades by hand over the sides of their open cockpits and shoot at enemy pilots with pistols and guns.

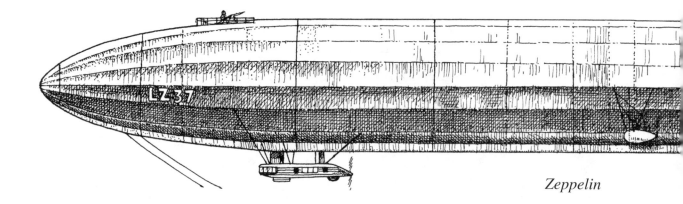

Zeppelin

New Inventions

As the war progressed, planes became larger, faster combat weapons.

The German *Fokker* triplanes were superior to the Allied airplanes. Their perfection of an interrupter gear in 1915 revolutionized the air war. Machine guns were mounted in front of the pilots. They were synchronized to fire bullets through the propeller's axle without damaging the blades. In 1915 and 1916, Britain and France lost air supremacy. They copied the secret of synchronized firing only after they captured a *Fokker* EIII.

At the battle of Verdun in 1916, fighter planes swooped down on the infantry, spraying them with machine gun fire. The importance of air supremacy became obvious. Germany dominated the skies until late in 1917 when the British developed the *Sopwith Camel*. The *Sopwith Camel* got its name from the "hump" behind the engine where the guns were mounted. With great flexibility and agility, it turned sharply at high speeds.

In April 1918, the Germans produced the Fokker DVII. Although slower than the *Sopwith Camel*, it climbed better and recovered quicker from a dive. The German *Albatros* DV had twin machine guns and a black Iron Cross on

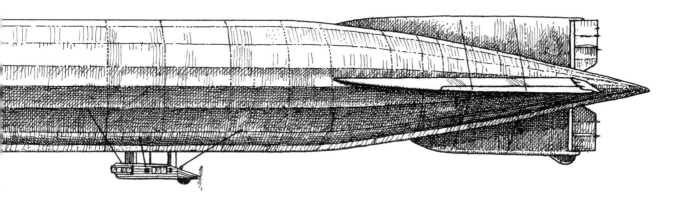

its wings. The Allies created the improved British *Sopwith Camel* SE5, and the French come out with the *Spad* XIII.

As their enemies produced better planes, the Germans changed their tactics from traditional one-on-one attacks to squadrons of eight to ten planes, called *Jagdstaffeln*, in order to outnumber their opponents.

Zeppelins

German Zeppelins were huge dirigible airships that travelled long distances to drop bombs. The largest L-Zeppelins had four motors, could fly for 100 hours, and drop 907 kg of bombs from 2280 m. They had an 18-man crew, including machine gunners, bombers, radio operators, pilots, and navigators. Zeppelins had no seats; crews stood on their feet at all times. If a Zeppelin became enshrouded in clouds, it lowered a small container, called a nacelle, on a cable. In the nacelle was an observer, who scanned the ground below and radioed information to the mother ship.

In 1915, the British created the *Sea Scout Zero* SSZ, a lightweight airship. It travelled at 72 km per hour, stayed 17 hours in the air, and had a crew of only three. It was used to escort convoys and to patrol for U-boats.

Sausages

Observation balloons were nicknamed Sausages. A defenceless radio observer swung far below the balloon on a long cable. The top speed of balloons was 80 km per hour. Filled with inflammable hydrogen gas, they burst into flames if hit by bullets or shells. Pilots went on Sausage shoots to explode observation balloons. It was a dangerous game. Only a highly skilled pilot could manoeuvre around the devastating blast that he caused.

Air Raids

The Germans were the first to invent planes that could drop bombs from above. The British and French quickly built their own. A technology war developed with bombers, as it had with fighter planes. The Germans designed airplanes called *Taubes* to raid French towns. To protect their terrorized citizens, the French developed the first anti-aircraft guns.

Aces and Dog Fights

A pilot's life was glorious but dangerous, and usually short. On average, a pilot joining the British Royal Flying Corps was dead within two weeks.

New vocabulary emerged. A "kill" was when a pilot destroyed an enemy plane, exploding it into flames in mid-air or sending it crashing to the ground. An Allied pilot who achieved five "kills" was declared an Ace. German pilots who scored 10 "kills" were called *Kanone*. Air battles were called dog fights, and could involve dozens of planes on both sides.

German pilots patrolled the skies over the trenches twice a day. They often travelled in groups called circuses. Allied pilots were usually loners flying from dusk to dawn on "hunting" patrols. If a fighter pilot encountered an enemy plane, he flew directly at his adversary, keeping him in his gun sights. Their engagements were very personal, one-on-one contests. They charged at

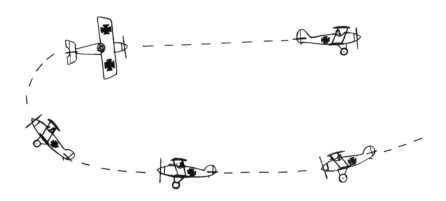

one another in a duel to the death. One trick was to get behind the opponent and attack from above or below.

A German, Max Immelman, invented the daring Immelmann turn. When he discovered an enemy behind him, he did a flying loop-the-loop to out-manoeuvre his opponent and get behind him. Other pilots copied and perfected the Immelmann turn. Those who didn't died.

Top 12 Aces of the Great War	
Baron Manfred von Richthofen (Germany)	80 victories - died in war at age 25
Paul René Fonck (France)	75 victories - survived the war
Billy Bishop (Canada)	72 victories - survived the war
Ernst Udet (Germany)	62 victories - survived the war
Edward "Mick" Mannock (England)	61 victories - died in war at age 30
Raymond Collishaw (Canada)	60 victories - survived the war
James McCudden (England)	57 victories - died in war at age 23
Donald MacLaren (Canada)	54 victories - survived the war
Andrew Beauchamp-Procter (South Africa)	54 victories - survived the war
Georges Guynemer (France)	54 victories - died in war at age 22
Erich Lowenhardt (Germany)	54 victories - died in war at age 21
Billy Barker (Canada)	50 victories - survived the war

Media Idols

Pilots on both sides became celebrities. These heroes were called Knights of the Sky, a comparison to medieval knights on horseback jousting in deadly contests. Civilians kept track of their heroes' victories as eagerly as hockey fans follow scoring records today.

Unlike soldiers in the trenches who watched from the mud below, pilots returned to their bases after each mission. Most were young, in their late teens or early twenties. They slept in soft beds, ate at expensive restaurants, and attended wild parties late into the night. They were praised by politicians, chased by adoring fans, and honoured with medal after medal. But only a few, the very skilled and the very lucky, survived the war. Most died horrendous deaths as their planes exploded or crashed.

Bloody April

The air slaughter peaked in April 1917 during the second battle of Arras. The Royal Flying Corps lost one-third of its force in intense dog fights, and a pilot's life expectancy became only days. The British outnumbered the Germans three to one, but they lost 316 pilots. German aces were more experienced and had superior planes.

The Red Baron

The best fighter pilot of the Great War was a German, Baron Manfred von Richthofen. He tallied a total of 80 victories. Because his *Fokker* triplane was painted a bright, blood red, he became legendary as the Red Baron.

Like most pilots on both sides, he abhorred being a hunter trying to increase his record of victories. He claimed sadly, "I am in wretched spirits after every battle." Exhausted from many years of flying and fighting, he was shot down in 1918 by an inexperienced Canadian pilot, Roy Brown.

Billy Bishop

As a boy, Billy Bishop hunted with his rifle in the woods near his home in Owen Sound, Ontario. He became skilled at hitting moving targets. This talent later made him the best Ace in the British Flying Corps.

When the Great War began, Billy joined the Canadian Expeditionary Force, but later transferred to the British Flying Corps. On March 25, 1917, flying a *Nieuport Scout*, he shot down his first enemy plane. Two weeks later, he received the Military Cross for destroying an observation balloon and another fighter plane. By April 20, with five victories, he had earned the title of Ace. In the trenches, infantrymen cheered the dog fights above.

On May 2, 1917, as he flew high over the front line, Billy spotted five enemy planes below him. He instantly descended, blasted two of them out of the sky, and chased the others away. For that, Billy received the Distinguished Service Order, a great honour for a junior officer.

On June 2, 1917, Billy, nicknamed the Lone Hawk, awoke before dawn and flew alone 20 km into enemy territory. There, he attacked a German airport. Three enemy planes rose to stop him, but he destroyed them. Britain gave Billy its highest award, the Victoria Cross, for his bravery on that day. In August, Billy's victories reached 47.

Promoted to a major, Billy Bishop was given the safer job of instructing new pilots on the art of surviving in the chaos of a dog fight. However, he became restless for the excitement and danger of combat.

Billy returned to the war in the spring of 1918 in command of his own squadron, called the Flying Foxes. He was only 24 years old. Within 12 days, he shot down 25 German planes and was awarded the Distinguished Flying Cross. The French government presented him with the *Legion d' Honneur* and the *Croix de Guerre*. Billy Bishop shot down 72 aircraft. Five were on his last day at the front.

One Against Sixty

Bill Barker learned to ride horses and shoot game on the Canadian prairies near his home town of Dauphin, Manitoba. The young hunter became proficient at shooting birds in flight.

As a corporal in the Canadian Rifles, he mastered the machine gun. He transferred to the British Air Corps early in 1916. Bill soon proved his skill with a Lewis machine gun. After two instruction flights, he qualified as a fighter pilot. He was given a plane and the rank of captain.

Above Italy, the Austrian air force ruled the skies from the Alps to the plains of Lombardy until late in 1917. In that year, Barker led Allied pilots in their new *Sopwith Camels* and took complete control of the air.

Disobeying orders against penetrating too deep into Austrian-held territory, Bill led a Christmas Day surprise attack. His squadron bombed mess halls and pulverized planes on the runways. Bill skimmed down, his wheels bouncing off the ground, and sent volleys of bullets into open hangar doors. During another raid, he sprayed machine gun fire on the Austrian headquarters. He also bombarded the enemy with thousands of leaflets, daring the Austrian pilots to come up and duel. By September 1918, the Canadian Ace had become a legend with 40 victories.

When Barker was ordered back to England to become an instructor for new pilots, he was unhappy about leaving combat. As he was returning to England in his *Sopwith Snipe*, he spotted a German reconnaissance plane. With hunter instincts, he stalked his prey and fired a machine gun burst. The enemy exploded in mid-air.

As Bill veered to continue his voyage, bullets suddenly tore through the side of his cockpit, shattering his right thigh. A German *Fokker* had caught Bill off guard. He lost consciousness as his plane fell 610 m in a death spin. The Ace regained control, picked up the enemy in his sights, and fired a hail of bullets that sent it down in flames. He watched his foe falling in a cloud of dark smoke, but bullets again showered his *Snipe*. Three squadrons of German fighters were stacked in the air above him. He was facing over 60 *Fokkers*. He destroyed three more of them, but another bullet penetrated his left thigh. Both legs were useless.

He fainted again and went into another fall until a gust of fresh air in the open cockpit revived him. He shot down a fifth enemy plane. But a German pilot also got off a few rounds. Bill's throttle arm shattered at the elbow. Again he lost conciousness, falling 1520 m before recovering.

With only one arm, he operated his control stick and firing button, destroying another enemy before turning to escape. Blocking his exit were more *Fokkers*. He fought off the new attackers and crash-landed behind British lines. Dazed and bleeding, he crawled from the bullet-riddled *Snipe* that lay upside down in the mud. He had shot down 6 of over 60 enemy triplanes before they defeated him.

Billy Barker lived to fly again. His victories rose to 50. He was awarded the Victoria Cross, the Distinguished Service Order, the Military Cross, France's *Croix de Guerre*, and Italy's Silver Medal for Military Valour.

Practical Jokers

While attacking a French air field, a German pilot lost one of his expensive, fur-lined leather gloves. The following day, he returned to the same spot and tossed the second one after its lost companion. An Allied pilot found them and dropped a thank you note on the German air field.

On another occasion, English pilot L.A. Strange bombarded a German air base with soccer balls as a prank.

66

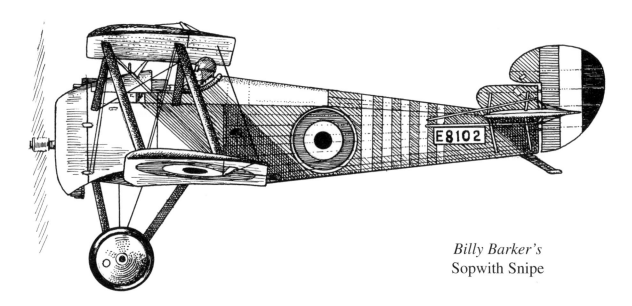

Billy Barker's
Sopwith Snipe

No Parachutes!

Building a plane was very expensive. British pilots were forbidden to carry parachutes because that would force them to try to save their planes. One famous Ace, Mick Mannock, carried a pistol so that he could kill himself quickly if his plane was hit and caught on fire.

Eyeballing

The term "eyeballing" came into use during the Great War. When a plane was hit, the victor swooped down and flew past his falling adversary, "eyeballing" him with a steady stare as a final salute of respect before the pilot and his plane crashed in flames.

Targeting and Observation

Here's a game that tests your ability to hit a target. Each team has two players, the shooter and the observer. The shooter tosses the bean bag over the screen, and the observer shouts out the position of the hit. Ring A (the bull's eye) is worth 5 points; Ring B is worth 4 points; Ring C is worth 3 points; Ring D is worth 2 points; Ring E is worth 1 point. The first team to get 100 points wins the game.

What you need:
- a screen: sheets or blankets hung from a clothes line or volleyball net
- 4 bean bags or old socks filled with sand
- chalk to draw a target

68

What to do:

1. With the chalk, draw a target 4 metres in diameter. Add the inner rings and bull's eye.
2. Set up the screen so that the shooter cannot see the target on the other side of the screen.
3. One member of the first team is the shooter and the other is the observer. The shooter throws the bean bag over the screen, and the observer shouts out the position on the target. For example, Ring E at 9 o'clock.
4. After three shots, the observer becomes the shooter. And then it's the next team's turn.

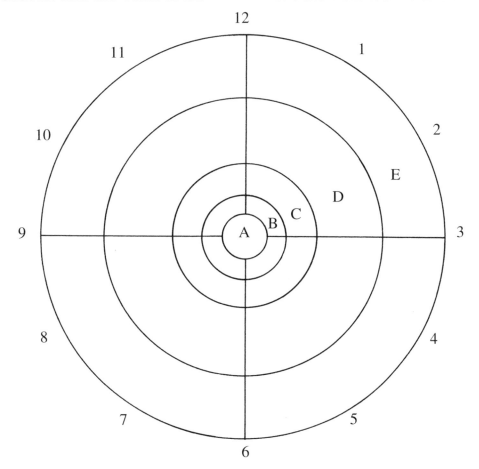

7 *The Final Years*

Julian Byng, Arthur Currie, and Others

At the start of the Great War, most people thought it would be over quickly and produce heroes and glorious victories. By the third year, hopes of adventure and excitement had turned to misery as soldiers faced the horrors of war in mud-filled trenches.

Most of the 32,000 original Princess Pats had become casualties. Hundreds of thousands of other Canadian troops had arrived in France to fight.

When the Russian Revolution eliminated the Eastern Front, Germany concentrated its attack in the West. In 1916-1917, the Germans fought the French for 10 months at Verdun, causing 250,000 casualties. By April 1917, the powerful U.S. had joined the Allies and declared war on Germany.

Hindenburg Line

Generals on both sides in the Great War believed that, once a position had been captured, it had to be defended at all costs. That idea caused hundreds of thousands of unnecessary deaths as troops captured, lost, and recaptured the same few metres of land.

In 1916-1917, the Germans tried a new strategy. Using Russian prisoners as labourers, they built the Hindenburg Line behind their front line trenches. It had 160 km of deep trenches protected by concrete walls, barbed wire, machine gun nests, and artillery. Troops were moved behind the Hindenburg Line for safety until it was time to deploy them.

Vimy Ridge (April 9, 1917)

For the Allies, occupying Vimy Ridge was a crucial objective on the Western Front. The nine-mile ridge was a German stronghold that dominated the countryside with three lines of tunnels, dug-outs, and machine gun nests protected by concrete and barbed wire. A French assault in 1915 was unsuccessful, with horrible losses. In 1916, a British attempt failed. The Canadians were ordered to capture Vimy Ridge in April 1917.

Canadian artillery ravaged enemy positions for a week. Then on Easter Monday, in a blinding snowstorm, all four of the Canadian divisions moved forward. Enemy snipers targeted them. The 1st, 2nd, and 3rd Divisions fought fiercely, in hand-to-hand combat, and reached their goal.

The 4th Division attacked Hill 145, the highest point on Vimy. After two days of huge losses, the troops conquered the ridge, except for the "pimple" on the north peak. The Germans rushed in reinforcements. On April 12, the Canadians and British 1st Corps advanced in freezing sleet and blinding snow. The Germans were overwhelmed and retreated.

Canadians captured Vimy. It was the first victory in two and a half years of combat. The unified Canadian force took more territory and prisoners than had been taken in any previous British battles. At the cost of 10,602 casualties, Canadians gained a new national pride.

Battles of Arras (April-May 1917)

Vimy Ridge was part of General Haig's larger plan of attack. The British fought four battles of Arras along the Scarpe River. They were designed to support a French attack that stalled and ended with a great loss of life.

The first battle, at Bullecourt, was an attempt to break through the Hindenburg Line. The German counter-attack captured tanks, and the Australian 4th Division was slaughtered. It ended on April 14.

The second battle began in late April. Canadians took their target, the Arleux Loop, an area between two British positions.

During the third offensive, from May 3 to May 4, Canadians had heavy casualties, but captured and held the village of Fresnoy. Allied attacks elsewhere failed, except for the Australians who took Bullecourt.

When the Canadian 1st Division rested on May 5, British soldiers replaced it at Fresnoy. The Germans attacked and retook the town. It was the last of the battles of Arras.

General Currie suggested a series of raids, striking German positions, then quickly falling back. They worked. The raids distracted the enemy and the British Second Army successfully attacked Messines on June 7, 1917.

General Arthur William Currie

General Byng was promoted to command the British Third Army. General Haig appointed Arthur Currie to command the Canadian Corps. Currie was the first Canadian to be commander of the Canadian troops.

Arthur Currie was born in Napperton, Ontario, in 1875. When he was a teenager, he moved to British Columbia. He became a teacher and a businessman. He joined the army militia and rose in rank to general.

General Currie never lost a fight. He turned the Canadian divisions into a serious fighting force. Currie was a rebel who followed his instincts. He refused to use old-school military strategies, which often resulted in the waste of soldiers' lives. He ignored orders that put his men at risk, suggesting better plans instead. He completed all missions assigned to him. His innovative military strategies were copied by the French and English.

Hill 70 (August 15, 1917)

The Germans captured Lens, the hub of France's coal industry in 1914. Many

Allied attempts to free the city failed. In 1917, the Canadians were given what appeared to be the impossible task.

It was General Currie's first challenge. He targeted Hill 70, the high ground north of the city, with hit-and-run raids and artillery bombardments, including gas shells. Machine guns blasted the enemy before the infantry advanced. Engineers lobbed drums of burning oil at the German defenders.

Determined not to be pushed out, the Germans responded with mustard gas and poured reinforcements into Lens. In three days of battle, 5800 Canadians became casualties. Four Victoria Crosses were awarded to Canadians, three to dead heroes. Hill 70 was captured. Canadians controlled the heights, but Lens remained in German hands until the next year.

Passchendaele (October 26, 1917)

The Canadians were ordered to conquer the strategic town of Passchendaele in Flanders. British forces had tried for a month but lost 68,000 men. Haig wanted to split the Canadians, but Currie insisted they fight as a team. He confronted General Haig, demanding that the attack be delayed until the roads and battlefield were prepared in order to reduce casualties.

Bombardments and sneezing gas combined with mustard gas hampered Canadians who were repairing roads and creating forward lines. Casualties grew to 1500 before the attack began. Concrete walls that were five feet high protected the enemy who had dug into the ridge above Passchendaele.

The Canadian 3rd and 4th Divisions attacked first. They lost 2500 men in three days. On October 30, 2300 more men became casualties. The 1st and 2nd Divisions replaced them on November 5. The next morning, Passchendaele was captured within three hours, but with another 2200 casualties. The ridge still remained in enemy hands.

Four days later, in drenching rain, the third battle of Ypres at Passchendaele

ended. It had taken 28 days of fighting, but they finally captured the ridge. The victory had claimed almost 16,000 Canadian casualties.

Canadian Cavalry at Cambrai (November 20, 1917)

The British attacked Cambrai to test their tanks and cavalry. On November 20, with aircraft support, 376 tanks roared forward in a line 10 km wide and penetrated 5 km of territory. Enemy fire destroyed 65 tanks; 114 suffered mechanical breakdowns.

The Canadian Cavalry Brigade led a charge involving thousands of horses and sabre-swinging riders. The men of the Fort Garry Horse swooped down on enemy artillery and infantry, causing chaos. The Canadian squadron leader fell dead; Lieutenant Harcus Strachan took over.

When night came, the Canadians were lost. As enemy soldiers approached them on all sides, they dismounted, scattered their horses, drew their swords, and fought their way back on foot. Only 40 survived, but they captured 16 prisoners. Lieutenant Strachan received a Victoria Cross.

The thundering tank attack proved the value of the new machines, but the Germans retaliated and retook the territory they had lost.

German Offensive (March 1918)

The Germans moved thousands of troops from the Eastern and Italian Fronts to the Western Front. They were desperate to win a major victory before the large American army of "Doughboys"* arrived.

The Canadian Corps was at Lens, part of the British First Army. All winter the Canadians reinforced their defences, building 400 km of trenches, which were protected by 500 km of barbed wire, 320 km of tunnels, and machine guns. The defences were designed to protect 16 km of front line.

Hidden behind a thick fog, the mighty German army launched its offensive. The British retreated in confusion. German troops surged after them, conquering 40 km of territory.

The Canadian 1st and 2nd Divisions were sent to reinforce the British Third Army. General Currie told his soldiers: "you will advance or fall where you stand ... those who will fall ... will not die but step into immortality. Your mothers ... will be proud to have borne such sons."

Motors to the Rescue

Raymond Brutinel, now a general, had prepared the Canadian Motor Machine Gun Brigade for fast, mobile combat. It was needed desperately and was ordered to Amiens to face the advancing Germans. The Motors travelled 160 km

* "Doughboys" was a nickname of U.S. infantry soldiers. They were proud of their nickname.

Brutinel's Motors

and went into action the same day. They had 20 vehicles, 40 guns, 280 men, and 51 motorcycle scouts.

The Motors protected the retreating British by harassing the enemy. Using hit-and-run tactics, they splattered the enemy with blasts of fire, then sped off. They wreaked deadly havoc but suffered shocking losses. One skirmish left only 8 of 50 alive, with all officers dead except one, who lost his arm. New recruits were quickly trained to replace them.

Battle of Amiens (August 8-11, 1918)
The Germans recaptured territory that Canadians had secured earlier. They advanced 40 km, but were stopped outside Amiens. The Canadian Corps were in the middle of the counter-attack at Amiens. On their left were Australians; on their right was the French First Army.

The Germans were unprepared. Camouflaged by a morning fog and supported by aircraft, artillery, machine guns, tanks, and cavalry, the Canadians

descended on them. The battle was a bloodbath. Four Canadian divisions pushed back 15 German divisions and took over 22 km of land along a 9000-m front. They captured 9000 prisoners, 200 guns, and 1000 machine guns and trench mortars. The Canadians suffered 11,000 casualties. Another 2000 later became casualties in small skirmishes. General Byng described the assault as "the finest operation of the war."

Horses Against Machine Guns

In one raid, Lieutenant Harvey of the Lord Strathcona's Horse charged and captured enemy troops that out-numbered his own force by three to one. At

Amiens, Lieutenant Gordon Flowerdew led the cavalry in an assault against a nest of machine guns. They attacked the enemy with their sabres. Flowerdew, who received a Victoria Cross for bravery, died in the action.

Attack on the Hindenburg Line (August-October 1918)

After Amiens, the Canadians were transported to the Arras sector with orders to smash through the indestructible Hindenburg Line and occupy Cambrai. Three heavily defended lines had to be conquered to achieve the goal. German intelligence warned that "the Canadians, the best British troops," were positioned at the Scarpe River. The Germans waited for them.

Fresnes-Rouvroy Line (August 1918)

On August 26, the attack began. It took two days of heavy fighting for the Canadians to reach the first fortification, the Fresnes-Rouvroy Line.

The Canadian soldiers trudged through thick mud and swam across the Sensée River. Fighting hand-to-hand in waist-high water, they were forced back twice. On the third attempt, they took the opposite river bank. Countless troops and all the officers were lost. The medical doctor took command, but also became a casualty. All but 70 of the 600 Canadians were wounded or killed. By August 31, they had captured the Fresnes-Rouvroy Line.

Drocourt-Quéant Line (September 1918)

The next obstacle on the road to Cambrai, the Drocourt-Quéant Line, was more heavily defended. Exhausted, but feeling victorious, the Canadian 1st and 4th Divisions advanced in lightning and thunder that was as loud as their artillery support. They captured 8 km along a 6400 m front at a cost of 5600 casualties to conquer the Drocourt-Quéant Line.

The Canadian 2nd and 3rd Divisions replaced the battle-ravaged 1st and 4th Divisions at the Canal du Nord, the last defence of Cambrai. The Allied commander, General Ferdinand Foch, ordered an attack along the entire Western Front: the Belgians in Flanders; the British (including the Canadians) at Cambrai; the French at Mézières; and the newly arrived American Doughboys at Argonne-Meuse.

Changing Plans

General Haig ordered the Canadians to make a frontal attack to aid the British Army as it captured Cambrai. General Currie considered it a suicide mission. He discovered a narrow passage across the canal, far to the south. He proposed a quick, sneak attack, scrambling the Canadian troops across the canal to surprise the enemy from behind. It was a brilliant plan, but dangerous. If discovered, they would be slaughtered. But Currie prevailed.

Canal du Nord (September-October 1918)

The Canadians secretly relocated close to the narrow crossing chosen by Currie. On September 27, they dashed across the dry canal bed and crawled up the opposite bank. The Germans awoke too late. The 1st Division troops uprooted their positions, allowing the British to cross the canal. The 4th Division assaulted the enemy in the village of Bourlon, but the British Third Army, accompanied by the Canadian 3rd Division, was slowed down by heavy resistance. Without its support, the Canadian 4th Division was vulnerable. The men were mowed down by machine guns. The battle raged for four bloody days. Torrents of rain soaked the Canadians as positions were captured, lost, and captured again. But General Currie's plan succeeded.

The Germans evacuated Cambrai. Between August 28 and October 11, Canadians progressed 37 km, engaged 31 enemy divisions, and freed 54 villages. There were 30,806 Canadian casualties.

The end of the Great War was finally in sight. Bulgaria, Austria-Hungary, and Turkey had surrendered to the Allied forces by October 1918, but the proud German army was determined to fight to the death.

General Arthur Currie

Pursuit to Valenciennes (October 1918)

The Canadian Cavalry Brigade galloped through villages in the Le Cateau area, facing machine guns and artillery. They penetrated 13 km and took 400 prisoners. The 4th Division liberated the city of Demain.

The Germans headed for Valenciennes, looting, burning, and destroying as they withdrew. Bitter about defeat, they committed many atrocities. As Canadians freed communities, the people swarmed into the streets showering them with cheers and kisses. Soldiers shared food with hungry villagers, before pursuing their still dangerous enemy.

At Valenciennes, Canadians captured Mount Houy, allowing General McNaughton's artillery to bombard enemy positions below. The infantry attacked on November 1 before daybreak. The Germans abandoned the city, leaving 800 of their dead soldiers and 80 dead Canadians.

The Allies moved forward from the North Sea to Verdun. Rain washed away roads, hampering the advancing infantry, supply vehicles, and civilians struggling to escape the battle zones. The Royal Canadian Engineers laboured to keep routes open. The new challenge was to feed thousands of starving refugees, who blocked the roads as they fled to safety.

Mons (November 10-11, 1918)

After Valenciennes, the 4th Division troops were given a rest. The 2nd Division replaced them with orders to capture Mons. On November 10, the Canadians approached the Belgian city, encountering artillery and machine gun fire. By midnight, the enemy had deserted the area. The Royal Highlanders of Canada overcame the only remaining Germans.

Citizens jumped from their beds and ran into the streets, celebrating their rescue. They had suffered four years of occupation, which began after the first battle of Mons. Only one Canadian died at Mons.

General Foch hand-picked Canadians to lead the final Allied attack in the last 100 days of the war. They defeated 64 German divisions.

The Great War officially ended at 11 a.m. on the 11th day of the 11th month. Canadians pledged to never forget the tragedies of war.

Versailles Treaty

The peace treaty, signed at Versailles, France, on June 28, 1919, was useless. It led to another world war 20 years later. When the Second World War started, the Great War became known as the First World War.

Death Count

About 628,000 Canadian men served in the Great War; 233,000 lost arms or legs, were blinded, or poisoned; and 59,544 died.

In total, 65 million soldiers fought in the war, and more than half became casualties. The bloodbath killed 8 million; 2 million suffered from illness and disease; 21.2 million were wounded; and 7.8 million were taken prisoner or listed as missing. About 9 million civilians died from starvation, disease, artillery fire, and air raids.

Pandemic

In the final 100 days of the Great War, another tragedy struck. In 1918, the Spanish flu spread throughout the world and infected about a billion people (half the world's population). It killed 25-40 million people world-wide, including 50,000 Canadians.

Casualties of the Great War (1914-1918)

Country	Dead	Wounded
Germany	1.8 million	4 million
Russia	1.7 million	
France and Empire	1.4 million	4.3 million
Austria-Hungary	1.2 million	
Great Britain and Empire*	1 million	2 million
Canada	59,544	233,000
Italy	600,000	
Ottoman Empire	400,000	
Romania	336,000	
U.S.	126,000	
Bulgaria	87,000	
Serbia	45,000	
Belgium	13,700	
Portugal	7,200	
Greece	5,000	*Canada is included
Montenegro	3,000	in the British Empire
Japan	300	

Native Hero

Francis Pegahmagabow was the most decorated Native soldier in the Canadian army in the Great War. An Ojibwa from the Parry Island Reserve in Ontario, he served as a scout and sniper with the 1st Division. He carried crucial messages and was seriously wounded two times. He captured 300 enemy soldiers and shot 378. He was awarded the Military Medal three times for courage under fire at the Somme, Passchendaele, and Ypres.

The Dumbbells

In the face of death and destruction, it was important for the troops to relax and laugh. Among the entertainment units in the war, the Canadian troupe known as the Dumbbells was unique. It put on shows for the soldiers.

Captain Merton Plunkett, an entertainment officer supplied by the YMCA, was assigned to the Canadian 3rd Division in France. He organized 10 volunteers, including his younger brother Al, who had joined the army at 16. Choosing the red dumbbell insignia of the 3rd Division as their name, they boosted the morale of the soldiers. They sang popular songs and performed comedy skits, often dressed as women. When they were not entertaining, they acted as stretcher-bearers. Even 10 years after the war ended, the Dumbbells toured Canada and became international stars.

Lone Heroes

During the attack on the Hindenburg Line, Lieutenant Charles Rutherford of the 5th Canadian Mounted Rifles won a Victoria Cross when he single-handedly secured the village of Monchy. He captured a machine gun post, and then forced a second one to surrender. He took 45 prisoners. When Rutherford's own troops arrived, they took another 35 prisoners.

Another Victoria Cross was earned by Captain C.N. Mitchell at Cambrai as the enemy blew up bridges to delay the Allied advance. He charged across a bridge, shot 3 enemy soldiers, and captured 12 others as his men disabled the explosives that had been set to destroy the bridge.

Great War Crossword Puzzle

ACROSS

1. Germany and Austria-Hungary were called the _____ Powers.
5. Canada's innovative general of artillery.
6. Shorter name for the Canadian 1st Machine Gun Brigade.
8. Canadian rifle that was famous for jamming.
9. Canadian general who convinced the Allies of the importance of the machine gun.
11. General Byng claimed this battle in August 1918 was "the finest operation of the war."
15. Impregnable German line of defence built behind the front line.
20. Passenger ship sunk by a German U-boat.
22. When his army was slaughtered at this battle, General Samsonov committed suicide.
23. German pilot known as the Red Baron.
25. Canadian Ace who fought 60 enemy planes.
26. Ridge captured in 1917 by the Canadians.
28. Huge dirigible airships.
29. These bloody battles in 1916 created a million casualties and used tanks.
31. He became famous as _____ of Arabia.
32. Title given to an Allied pilot who shot down five enemy planes.
33. The Uncrowned King of Romania.
35. German cruisers that sank 47 Allied ships.
36. Soldiers on the Western Front lived in them.
38. Observation balloons filled with hydrogen gas.
39. Canada's top pilot in the Great War.
40. Only major sea battle in the Great War.

DOWN

1. Canadian-born general who commanded the Canadian Corps in the final years of the war.
2. Original name for a tank.
3. Early battle in 1914 where General von Rennenkampf won over Germany.
4. Ships formed these for protection from U-boats.
7. Canadian who later became a famous spy and the inspiration for James Bond.
10. This secret-coded telegram invited Mexico to join the war.
12. Americans changed this name to "liberty sandwich" during the Great War.
13. At this battle in October 1917, Canadians became victims of sneezing gas.
14. German name for a submarine.
16. This gear revolutionized machine gun fire in the air war.
17. Comedy group that entertained Canadian troops on the front line.
18. Peninsula where Turkish troops defeated the Allies in 1915.
19. Original name of this Canadian city before the Great War was Berlin.
21. The powers of Britain, France, and Russia.
24. His assassination started the Great War.
27. Prime Minister of Canada during the war.
28. Real name of the female spy Mata Hari.
30. The doctor who wrote "In Flanders Fields."
34. At this battle, Canadians encountered poison gas for the first time.
35. Country that created the Eastern Front.
37. Airplane with a "hump" that housed its guns.

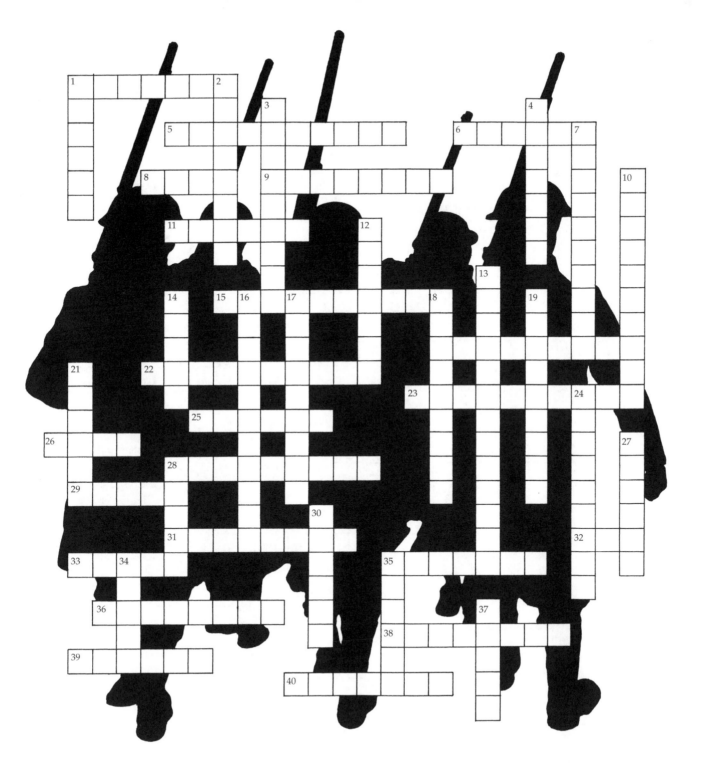

Across

1. CENTRAL
5. MCNAUGHTON
6. MOTOR
8. ROSS
9. BRUTINEL
11. AMIENS
15. HINDENBURG
20. LUSITANIA
22. TANNENBURG
23. RICHTHOFEN
25. BARKER
26. VIMY
28. ZEPPELINS
29. SOMME
31. LAWRENCE
32. ACE
33. BOYLE
35. RAIDERS
36. TRENCHES
38. SAUSAGES
39. BISHOP
40. JUTLAND

Down

1. CURRIE
2. LADDSHIP
3. GAMBINE
4. CONVOYS
7. STEPHENSON
10. ZIMMERMERM
12. HAMEL
13. PASIC
14. UBOOT
16. INTTERU
17. NUMBER
18. GALLPOLI
19. KIOR
21. ALLEVE
24. FERDINND
27. BORD
30. MCCRAE
34. YPTRE
37. CAMEL

88

Index